Summary of
A Gentleman in Moscow:
A Novel

Written by Amor Towles

Summarized
by
Brief Books

Note to readers:

This is an unofficial summary & analysis of *A Gentleman in Moscow: A Novel by Amor Towles*. It is designed to enrich your reading experience. We strongly encourage that you buy the original book.

Table of Contents

Book Summary

of

A Gentleman in Moscow: A Novel

A Gentleman in Moscow is an intricately crafted novel by Amor Towles that manages to tell a decades long story involving only a few main characters and one location – the Metropol Hotel in Moscow.

Count Alexander Ilyich Rostov is sentenced to permanent house arrest within the Metropol Hotel in 1922 because of he is considered a threat to the Communist Party. Upon being sentenced, the Count is forced to move from his lavish suite in the hotel up to the isolated 6th floor. Rather than dwelling on his new riches to rags situation, he chooses to embrace practicalities and foster the aesthetics that are central to his spirit.

While living in the hotel, he befriends the hotel staff and a young girl named Nina who also lives there. Nina opens Rostov's eyes to all the hotel offers. With her help, he learns about every corner of the hotel and learns the intricacies of hotel life. After Nina presents him with her secret hotel passkey, Rostov can explore any area he wants, and he discovers the hotel is a whole world itself.

Eventually, Rostov throws himself into working at the hotel's fine dining establishment, the Boyarsky, where he develops strong bonds with the maître d and the chef. Along the way, he also becomes involved in an intimate relationship with a hotel guest, the famous actress, Anna Urbanova.

While the years pass, Rostov has become acquainted with others and the world within the walls of the hotel, but his life takes a shocking turn when the grown-up Nina appears and asks him to take care of her daughter, Sofia. Rostov agrees and his life is never the same. Sofia becomes his daughter since her mother never returns, and Rostov now focuses his energy on raising her and working in the Boyarsky. The novel tells of their adventures and their unique relationship with each other and the rest of the staff at the hotel as Sofia grows up within these walls.

When Sofia is 13 years old, she suffers a serious accident, and Rostov leaves the hotel for the first time in many years to get her help. In the following years, Rostov marvels as Sofia becomes an accomplished pianist and an adult woman. As time has passed, he has grown closer to the actress and his friends at the restaurant. After celebrating Sofia's recent win at a music competition with Anna and his friends, he learns his longtime friend Mishka has passed away following years as a prisoner. It is revealed that the poem that landed Rostov under house arrest was actually written by Mishka. Rostov soberly reflects that they thought they were saving Mishka's life by lying about the poem's writer, when it was his life that was saved.

After Sofia is presented the opportunity to travel with the orchestra and hesitates because she does not want to leave him, Rostov concocts an elaborate escape plan to free him from the Metropol after decades of house arrest. He encourages Sofia's travel and his escape by masterfully involving several others without their full knowledge. After three decades in the Metropol, Rostov is able to escape and reunite with his love, Anna, outside of the hotel.

Setting Summary

of

A Gentleman in Moscow: A Novel

Moscow, 1922 – 1954

Russia in the year 1922 had just recovered from three major events: World War I, the Russian Civil War, and the Red Terror, which had ravaged the nation for nearly two decades. 1922 was also a notable as the USSR was formed during this time. While the novel begins in 1922, it continues through 1954 while Russian gradually transitions from communism to state capitalism.

Although the story takes place in Moscow, the majority of the story takes place within **The Metropol** hotel located within the city. This world-famous hotel serves as the true setting for the novel because this is where the main character is sentenced to life imprisonment. Within the Metropol, the audience will also become familiar with specific areas of the hotel:

- **The Boyarsky**: This is a fine dining restaurant located within the hotel where Rostov dines nightly and where he eventually works as head waiter.

- **The Piazza**: This is a portion of the hotel that is modeled after a little country where guests can eat, drink, listen to the orchestra and people watch.

- **The Shalyapin**: This is the hotel bar where Rostov has a nightly drink and where many guests strike up conversations.

- **Suite 317**: Rostov's first room before his life imprisonment on the 6th room. This suite is central to the novel's plot and character development.

- **Idlehour**: Rostov grew up on this estate located within Nizhny Novgorod (Russia's 5th largest city). This area is known for its delicious apples. Rostov often reflects on his time here.

Character List

of

A Gentleman in Moscow: A Novel

Main Characters

- Count Alexander Ilyich Rostov – main character of the novel

- Nina Kulikova – young girl also living at the hotel

- Anna Urbanova – the movie star and Rostov's lover

- Sofia – Nina's daughter/adopted by Rostov

Secondary Characters

- Andrey Duras – the maître d of the Boyarsky

- Mikhail Fyodorovich Mindich (Mishka) – close lifelong friend

- Emile Zhukovsky – chef of the Boyarsky

- Arkady – front desk clerk

- Helena – Rostov's deceased sister

- Vasily – hotel's concierge

- Marina – seamstress

- Konstantin Konstantinovich – lender

- Yaroslav Yaroslavl – barber

- Audrius – bartender

- Jozef Halecki – hotel manager

- Katerina Litvinova – Mishka's love

- The Bishop/Leplevsky – a waiter/manager at the hotel; Rostov's nemesis

- Abram – the handyman

- Osip Ivanovich Glebnikov – officer of the Party sent to watch Rostov

- Martyn – waiter

- Richard Vanderwhile – American Captain in the intelligence field

- Viktor Stepanovich Skadovsky – conductor of the orchestra in the Piazza

- Professor Matej Sirovich – famous Russian poetry professor

- Pudgy Webster – American who aids Rostov

- Boris – barber

Chapter Summary and Analysis

of

A Gentleman in Moscow: A Novel

Book One

1922: An Ambassador

After almost two decades of war, Rostov and the rest of the country rejoice at their newfound peace, but also face uncertainty for their future. The novel begins as Count Rostov is taken back to the hotel where he has been staying as a guest but now is forced to stay permanently under house arrest. He is moved from his lavish suite 317 to a much smaller room on the 6th floor. He can only take a few possessions. He chooses to take his sister's scissors, his grandfather's desk (with hidden gold pieces in the legs), brandy, his father's books, and his grandmother's porcelain dishes. Upon settling into his new permanent room, he celebrates his return with the hotel staff.

An Anglican Ashore

A quote that his godfather had once told him has resonated with Rostov to this day: "If a man does not master his circumstances, then he is bound to be mastered by them." Rostov decides to master his circumstances through practicalities, and this very philosophy spurs him to make the best out of his current condition. He gets to work making his room less cluttered and more accommodating. He then has a meeting with Konstantin Konstantinovich and has the gold he has hidden verified. Upon verifying it, he agrees to the Count's requests. The Count requested three items – fine bed linens, soap, and a French pastry.

An Appointment

Rostov begins his day determined to make the most out of his time by finally starting on his father's favorite book. However, Rostov's weekly appointment with the hotel barber is the true highlight of his day, and his excitement is apparent in his lack of focus with reading. At the barber shop, Rostov upsets a man by taking his place despite the man arriving before him. Rostov displays a lack of awareness on the social gaffe he has committed, and pays for it when the incensed man maims Rostov's moustache. Despite it all, Rostov continues to be reflective and sees a silver lining to everything.

An Acquaintanceship

Count Rostov meets a precocious, nine-year-old girl named Nina Kulikova who inquires about his missing mustache. While sharing his lunch with her, he is charmed by her discussion of princesses and duels. After this conversation, it causes the Count to reflect on duels throughout history that evening while he drinks in the Shalyapin. Despite having stayed in the Metropol for over four years, Rostov develops a keener eye and has new observations of his surroundings. The hotel has seen better, glorious days, much like Rostov fully embracing a pampered life before the war.

Anyway...

Nina, a fanciful child who dreams of being a princess, takes it upon herself to learn etiquette from Rostov five days later. Rostov, having never been particularly good with children, treats Nina as befitting her surprising maturity, and the two get along well.

Around and About

As Rostov and Nina begin their daily adventures by exploring the Metropol together, he rediscovers the same building despite having stayed there for years. Nina becomes the teacher and he the student, acquainting him with all the secrets and stories the Metropol has to offer. With Nina's secret passkey to the hotel, they can explore all the rooms in the hotel. As he finds a new tenant--a gentleman like him--staying in his old room, a wistful sadness comes over him. However, inspired by Nina's sense of adventure and discovery, Rostov finds an ingenious way to secretly expand his living quarters. He creates a secret entrance into the closed off room beside his room through his closet. He now has his bedroom for his practicalities and his hidden study for his spirit.

An Assembly

Nina convinces Rostov to spy on an assembly of the Second Meeting of the First Congress of the Moscow Branch of the All-Russian Union of Railroad Workers. Crouched and hidden on the balcony, they observe a heated disagreement over which verb should be used in the sentence – finally settling on "enable and ensure" over "facilitate." After tearing his pants as a result, Rostov must get them mended by Marina where he reflects on Nina's fast disinterest in princesses. Then, he is asked to meet with the hotel manager. When in the manager's office, he discovers a hidden cabinet behind a frame.

Archaeologies

Before he can finish his card tricks in the Shalyapin one evening, the bartender interrupts him to let him know a pacing man requests him. This pacing man turns out to be the Count's longtime friend from his university days in St. Petersburg, Mikhail Fyodorovich (Mishka). He comes with news of the new poetry movement in Russia and the RAPP (the Russian Association of Proletarian Writers).

Advent

It is Christmas season at the hotel. Rostov and Nina have a special dinner together and eat ice cream. He gives her his grandmother's opera glasses. She presents him with a gift he is not to open until midnight. He is surprised to find Nina has presented him with her secret hotel passkey. While a festive chapter, Book One ends with the narrator suggesting Rostov's Ghost of Christmas Future would show him trying to kill himself four years later.

Book Two

1923: An Actress, an Apparition, an Apiary

It is the one-year anniversary of Rostov's permanent entrance into the hotel for his arrest. He has a meeting with his friend, Mishka, and then has an encounter with a willowy woman struggling with her two dogs. She later invites him to dinner in her suite where he learns she is a famous actress named Anna Urbanova. She takes the lead, and they end up sleeping together. Upon leaving her room, Rostov feels ghostlike and contemplates spirits. He goes to investigate the weird breeze he felt and discovers a ladder to the roof. He climbs the ladder and meets the hotel's handyman, Abram, who gives him coffee and a slice of bread with honey from his beehives. They learn that they both lived in Nizhny Novgorod while discussing the delicious apples on the Chernik Estate.

Addendum

In this addendum, readers get the opportunity to hear Anna's reaction to her evening with Rostov. She finds she cannot stop thinking about him picking up her blouse off the floor and hanging it up before leaving her room. She grows angrier as time passes because she feels it was a slight to her and she can treat her own clothing however she wants. She takes to permanently removing her clothes and leaving them piled on the floor. When her dresser, Olga, confronts her, Anna throws all her piled-up clothing into the street. Olga points out how her neighbors will think she is a petulant actress, so Anna sneaks out into the night to retrieve her garments.

1924: Anonymity

Rostov begins to feel as if he is slowly becoming invisible to the people in the hotel. Nina is preoccupied with her studies. Then, his friend, Mishka, cannot meet him for dinner. When he decides to proceed to dinner alone, he is shocked to learn the Bishop (an inexperienced waiter from the Piazza) has been promoted to a waiter in the Boyarsky. He attempts to order a specific type of wine from the Bishop, who simply repeatedly asks if he would like "red wine" instead of identifying the type by name. He goes to Andrey, the maître d of the Boyarsky, only to discover the Bishop has been promoted because he has friends with influence. Furthermore, the Bishop has filed a complaint about the Boyarsky's wine list because he feels it runs counter to the ideals of the revolution. Thus, the Boyarsky now only sells nonlabelled "red" or "white" wine. Andrey shows Rostov the wine cellar with all the labels having been removed. However, the chapter ends with Rostov being able to identify a certain bottle based on the insignia on the glass and taking it foreshadowing 1926 when he will drink it and try to end his life.

1926: Adieu

Rostov's philosophy based on weather and meteorology is given while telling a story about a fellow attending the 21st birthday of Princess Novobacky during which snow falls and leads to another fellow slipping on the ice – both men want the attention of the Princess. Since the one fellow cannot dance due to his sore tailbone, the other suggests a card game – and beats him soundly. After beating the already injured man, the other fellow decides to call it even and rips the man's IOU in two. The princess is so impressed with his gallantry that these two end up dancing and on the terrace. According to Rostov, this is all because of the weather and temperature. After this story is told, the novel returns to the present with Rostov searching for Nina (now 13 years old) in the ballroom. He finds her with a young man on the upper floor doing experiments to test theories of gravity and objects falling.

Later, as he eats dinner at the Boyarsky, readers learn that this is the evening Rostov plans to kill himself and that he has already put his plans in order – complete with a gold piece for the undertaker. After dinner, he heads to the Shalypin for a drink where he gets drawn into a conversation about the greatness of Russia. One of the drinking men asks him where he comes from and readers learn the story of the Princess's party is true, and Rostov is the man who humiliated the other fellow. The other fellow sought revenge on Rostov by courting his sister, Helena, humiliating her, and breaking her heart. Rostov shoots this man in the arm to defend his sister's honor and is sent to Paris as a result. While he was in Paris, his sister died of Scarlet Fever. He wishes he had been with her when she passed away, but blames it all on the weather and his choices at the party.

After this conversation, Rostov proceeds to the roof where he plans to jump (hence the foreshadowing of Nina's experiment), but his plan is interrupted by Abram, the handyman, who tells him the bees are back – and the honey tastes of the apples in Nizhny Novgorod. The chapter ends with Rostov returning to his room and returning the gold piece where readers are told it remains for 28 years.

Book Three

Rostov awakes and prepares his own coffee in his room and east breakfast. Upon placing the dishes in the hall, he finds an envelope with "4 'o clock?" written on it.

Arachne's Art

Readers learn Rostov is now the head waiter of the Boyarsky when the Count, Emile, and Andrey have their daily meeting. While at the meeting, Rostov shows the other two men what is in the envelope (saffron). The men discuss an exciting secret and are on the quest for oranges. When heading to his room, he runs into a grown-up Nina visiting the hotel with her work colleagues. She seems serious and very busy. He is so concerned about Nina's serious manner that he discusses it with Marina, the seamstress, while they repair buttons. The chapter ends with the Count going to suite 311 to find the willowy figure leaving a dress on the floor.

An Afternoon Assignation

Focusing on the reappearance of Anna Urbanova, readers learn of her downfall as an actress upon Stalin's disapproval of the types of films she appeared in and the invention of talking pictures with no place for her husky voice. She becomes a has-been. After this occurrence, she sees the Count a second time after a failed meeting with a young director at the hotel. They recognize each other as members of the Confederacy of the Humbled. However, Anna's fame begins to rise again (while her character is still humbled), and she continues her relationship with the Count.

An Alliance

Rostov is asked to attend a private meeting in the Boyarsky. It is here that he meets Osip Ivanovich Glebnikov – a former colonel of the Red Army and an officer of the Party. He is keeping tabs on interesting men such as the Count. However, he is there because he wants Rostov to help him learn to speak with the privileged classes of other countries by dining with him once a month.

Absinthe

Rostov procures some absinthe from the bartender, and we learn that it is for the Triumvirate's celebration (Rostov, Emile, and Andrey). The men have finally gathered all 15 ingredients needed to make bouillabaisse. They are almost thwarted by the Bishop, but Emile sends him away. At their special celebration, they eat their lavish feast, drink merrily, and talk of their past lives.

Addendum

Nina and her three confederates head to Ivanov with a sense of purpose to build power stations, steel mills and manufacturing plants. The country needed grain producing regions to do this part. But, the kulaks were exiled (essentially the farmers), and by 1932, it would result in widespread hardship for the agricultural provinces of Old Russia and death by starvation for millions of peasants in the Ukraine.

1938: An Arrival

As the novel skips ahead in time, readers are simply told the early thirties in Russia were unkind. Summer arrives and Rostov is surprised and delighted to when Nina comes by the hotel unexpectedly. He can tell it is for a personal reason. She tells him that her husband of six years has been arrested and sentenced to five years' corrective labor. She plans to go to him and needs Rostov to watch her daughter, Sofia, who is five years old, while she is away. This paramount conversation is over within fifteen minutes. Rostov agrees and Sofia goes with him.

Adjustments

Rostov is mystified by how much space little Sofia takes up and what he will talk to her about for all the hours in the day. After striking out with elephants and princesses, he discovers she is fascinated by his twice-chiming clock. They discuss the clock over lunch where the new waiter, Martyn, is a great help by pointing out that Sofia may need her veal cut and that she may need to use the restroom. Since Rostov has no experience with children, he is grateful for Martyn's gentle assistance.

Ascending, Alighting

When Rostov arrives at work, he thinks his friends are covering for his new situation with Sofia, but then realizes he has forgotten his monthly meeting with Osip. In the rush of the day, he almost forgets his appointment with Anna who he also tells about his new circumstances. Anna is understanding and allows him to borrow her luggage. He uses it to carry tomato cans upstairs to craft bunk beds.

On his way to pick up Sofia from Marina's, he runs into his friend, Mishka, who is furious when he is asked to cut out the parts of Chekhov's letters that refer to bread. Rostov is able to calm him down for the evening. Mishka ends up having a breakdown and storming into his editor's office. As a result, he ends up in Serbia after he is questioned regarding this episode.

The news about Sofia is found out by the government, but she is left alone because of her possible connection to a famous actress. Rostov begins to adjust to life with Sofia and learns how to talk with her.

Addendum

Sofia wakes up Rostov to tell him she left Dolly in Aunt Marina's room.

1946

On Saturday, June 25, 1946, lines upon lines upon lines of people continue to the entrance of Lenin's tomb. After all these years, the Germans did not make it into Moscow and many of the old facades remain the same, such as the Metropol Hotel.

Antics, Antithesis, an Accident

The Bishop is now the hotel manager and calls Rostov into his office to ask him about the events on the fourth floor early that morning. Three geese were loose on the hall and caused pandemonium (screaming, running, mistress sightings, the accidentally flashing of underwear, and women fainting). After being questioned, Rostov is furious that the Bishop seems to insinuate Sofia had something to do with it. After this meeting, the narrator describes a game Sofia plays where she can get around the hotel quickly without detection and appear calm and unfazed when she encounters the person she has surprised. Rostov discusses his conversation with the Bishop, with Emile, and with Andrey who agree it couldn't have been Sofia. But, then they tell him someone needs to clean the feathers out of the dumbwaiter.

The men's conversation is interrupted by a waiter who tells them a man who looks like a beggar is asking for Rostov. It is Mishka who Rostov has not seen in 8 years. Andrey and Emile welcome him with bread and salt (the Russian symbols of hospitality). Mishka tells his friend that he is working on a little project. Following this meeting with Mishka, Rostov attends his monthly meeting with Osip. They have switched from books to watching and discussing films.

After this meeting, Rostov visits the Shalypin where he has some drinks with a friendly American named Richard Vanderwhile. On his way to his suite, he sees Sofia in the lobby and decides to try to beat her at her own game. After rushing upstairs and seemingly beating her, he waits patiently. However, one of the chamber maids rushes in to tell him Sofia has fallen on the stairs. She is unconscious and bleeding. He picks her up and rushes out of the hotel for the first time in over 20 years to get a taxi to take her to a hospital. He asks the driver to take him to the only hospital he remembers, and upon arriving, quickly realizes this hospital is no longer the best. As he is starting to panic, the chief of surgery from a different hospital arrives to treat Sofia.

Sofia comes through the procedure, and while Rostov is waiting, he is shocked to see Osip arrive. He discovers it was Osip who arranged a more suitable surgeon, gets Sofia to a new hospital, and brings Marina to stay with her since Rostov must secretly return to the hotel of his imprisonment.

Addendum

On June 23, 1946, Andrey visits Sofia at the hospital and then returns to the small apartment he only shares with his wife. Readers learn their only child, Ilya, was killed in the Battle of Berlin. His room is kept the same, but Andrey knows once word gets out that they have an extra room, they will either have to move or get a roommate.

Book Four

1950: Adagio, Andante, Allegro

Sofia is now 17 years old, and Rostov recognizes that she has an
entirely different demeanor than her mother. She is demure. He
speaks with Vasily about her growing up and time passing when
Vasily tells him she is in the ballroom with Viktor Stepanovich
Skadovsky (conductor of the orchestra at the Piazza). Rostov rushes
into the ballroom and picks up Viktor by the lapels all while Sofia
and Viktor try to explain that nothing inappropriate is happening. He
is teaching her to play piano. To Rostov's surprise and delight, Sofia
is an extraordinary piano player and plays with feeling. He praises
her and asks her about how she plays with the feeling the way she
does. She confesses that she thinks about her mother to help with
mood. Moved, Rostov tells Sofia stories about Nina.

1952: America

Sofia and Rostov have dinner in the Boyarsky while Anna is also present at the restaurant. Anna is now a stage actress and can reside for months at a time at the Metropol. While they are eating, they are interrupted by the widely respected, Professor Matej Sirovich, who requests Rostov's presence in Suite 317 that evening. After this interruption, Sofia asks Rostov why they do not invite Anna to join them, and he is shocked to learn Sofia, Anna, and Marina have discussed it. When he visits his old suite for the first time in 25 years, he is surprised to see his friend, Richard, waiting there. He was the one to set up this private meeting to see if Rostov would be willing to relay information about Russia after Stalin's passing. Rostov refuses.

1953: Apostles and Apostates

Rostov, Anna, Andrey and Emile are celebrating Sofia's win at a concert competition in the secret study. Then, Andrey recalls the night they all toasted Rostov's permanent arrival to the sixth floor. At this point, Vasily appears through the closet door warning Rostov that the Bishop is on his way up. The Bishop introduces him to Frinovsky – the director of the Red October Youth Orchestra who plans to take Sofia to Stalingrad. Rostov senses the Bishop's role in this order, but before he can react, Anna steps out of the closet and lies about the Minister of Culture's interest in Sofia ending any discussion of her going to Stalingrad.

Back in the closet study, they all toast Rostov. As everyone goes to leave, he sees a woman waiting for him in the hall. This woman is Katerina Litvinova (Mishka's lover). Mishka has died and she came to tell Rostov in person. During their conversation, Rostov confesses Mishka wrote the poem that got Rostov imprisoned in the Metropol, and they lied to protect Mishka. But, Rostov suggests that the poem ended up saving him instead of Mishka. Katerina then presents Rostov with Mishka's final project – *Bread and Salt*. It is a compendium of quotes from seminal texts with the word **BREAD** capitalized and printed in bold.

Book Five

1954: Applause and Acclaim

The triumvirate are delighted to learn Sofia has the opportunity to visit Paris with the orchestra. After this discussion, the Bishop joins them for their daily meeting – which he does now to manage every detail. After the meeting, Rostov sneaks back to review the 1954 reservation book and notices that one June 11th the Boyarsky will be hosting dinner with two of the most powerful bodies in the Soviet Union. Related to this news, he retrieves a hidden gold piece from the leg in the desk. That evening in the Shalypin, he is met by a panicked Viktor Stepanovich telling him Sofia has passed on the opportunity to go to Paris with the traveling orchestra. Rostov speaks with Sofia and encourages her to leave the hotel and travel.

Achilles Agonistes

Rostov crafts a fake note to a barber named Boris from the hotel manager requesting the barber immediately. When the barber leaves for the fake meeting, Rostov is in the barbershop alone long enough to steal the "fountain of youth" and a razor blade. He is secretly preparing something for Sofia's departure in six months. He uses the razor to cut out a map of Paris and then begins removing the text from Montaigne's *Essays*.

Arrivederci

In Early May, Rostov watches a couple leave for a show and a late
dinner. He then uses Nina's hotel passkey to sneak into their room to
steal some clothing. Then, he visits the Shalypin and reviews his
checklist. He still needs "the matter of notice." After realizing the
boisterous American Pudgy Webster reminds him of his old friend
Richard, he thinks they may know each other from the intelligence
committee. Later, he sneaks into Webster's room, waits for him, and
then asks him to deliver a letter to Richard. After drinking some
more, he sneaks back into the couple's room hoping to steal the cap,
and he ends up getting stuck in their closet when they arrive home.

Adulthood

Rostov and Anna watch as Sofia models the beautiful dress Marina made her. Seeing her in the dress, they realize Sofia has clearly reached adulthood. However, when she turns around, Rostov objects to the low back that exposes her spine. In speaking out, he offends Marina. The women ignore his fatherly complaints. After this event, Rostov attends his daily meeting for the Boyarsky where he is disappointed to be removed from overseeing the dinner of the Presidium and the Council of Ministers as this was central to his secret plan. He pulls Andrey aside to discuss something in private at the end of the chapter.

An Announcement

Rostov does indeed end up overseeing the dinner on June 11th because Andrey has a terrible tremor in his hands, and he has already told comrade Propp that Headwaiter Rostov will assume his responsibilities. Propp meets with Rostov beforehand to go over all the details and tells him there will be no seating chart. Rostov recognizes that without a seating chart any studious observer will learn everything about the Russian government based on who seats where without any direction. In addition, Rostov can listen in on all the private conversations. The grand event at the dinner is the announcement from Malyshev that the first nuclear power plant will begin providing power to half the city of Moscow at 11pm that evening.

Anecdotes

Rostov has presented Sofia with all the items he has collected for her and told her what she must do the previous evening (the audience is still unaware). Tonight, he then takes Sofia through the closest where the secret study has been set up for a fancy dinner. They dine on soup and are served by Andrey. Rostov tells funny stories and they eat Goose 'a la Sofia. Rostov refrains from using the dinner as a time to provide fatherly advice and tells anecdotes instead. He then presents Sofia with the only picture he has of himself. Upon seeing the picture with his mustache, he recalls the brute cutting it and his friendship with Sofia's mother beginning as a result. He reveals that the only time in his life he needed to be at a particular time and place was when her mother brought her to him at the Metropol. At 10 'o clock, Marina arrives to escort Sofia to her train. The hotel staff all see her off. After she leaves, Rostov goes to his "empty nest," writes five letters and goes to bed.

An Association

Rostov and Osip have met less and less frequently, but when they see each other, Rostov suggests they meet to watch *Casablanca* together on June 19th. While watching the film, Osip is drawn into it and Rostov imagines Sofia arriving in Paris.

Antagonists at Arms (And an Absolution)

While serving in the Boyarsky, Rostov waits on a couple from Finland, and he hopes to steal the man's passport and Finnish currency. He is able to use his passkey to sneak into their room later that evening to retrieve the items. After, he heads to his room where he finds the Bishop sitting at the desk looking at the maps he has made of Paris. The Bishop leaves the room, but clearly has a plan. However, when the Bishop enters his own office, he is surprised to find Rostov sitting at his desk holding a gun. When Rostov arrived in the manager's office, he opened the longtime hidden cabinet behind a framed portrait that holds a gun. The two adversaries square off, but Rostov ultimately defeats the Bishop by showing him the gun is loaded and forcing him to hand over his set of keys. Rostov then leads the Bishop into the basement at gunpoint. There, he burns his personal files and forces the Bishop into the locked closet of curiosities that holds banquet materials.

Apotheoses

Rostov spends the next day following his practical routine until he left the Boyarsky and borrowed a raincoat and fedora from a guest. He then collected his small travel bad and bid adieu to his room. At this same time, Sofia is finishing playing her piece in Paris. After she finishes, she changes out of her beautiful dress into men's clothing, cuts her hair, dyes her white strip of hair with the "fountain of youth," and slips out the exit and into the night. She then arrives at the embassy to see Richard Vanderwhile, who was expecting her but did not know any details about when or how she would arrive. Richard presents her with a package that was waiting for her. Inside the package is Montaigne's *Essays*, but the pages have been cut out and eight stacks of gold coins are inside. Sofia then presents Richard with a knapsack he is told to cut into. Inside the bag is a rolled paper with all the details of the private conversations Rostov heard at the Combined Dinner of Council of Ministers and Presidium. In addition, there is a note requesting Richard to let Rostov know Sofia has made it safely to the embassy with a special instruction – he asks Richard to have several people call the Metropol's phone number at the same time. When all the phones begin to ring, chaos ensues and Rostov is able to walk out of the Metropol Hotel.

Afterword

Afterwords...

On the evening Rostov escaped the Metropol Hotel, Viktor Stepanovich Skadovsky leaves his apartment before midnight to meet Rostov in a café. After this meeting takes place, readers learn the KGB arrived at the Metropol Hotel to question Rostov, but discover no one knows where he is. After being questioned, Andrey and Emile are delivered letters from the postmaster (who also delivered letters to Marina, Audrius and Vasily). The letters are from Rostov telling them he has left the hotel and include gold pieces. After freeing the Bishop, everyone becomes aware that Sofia has also disappeared. Intelligence suggests Rostov is on the Finland and has headed to Vyborg. However, the previous evening, after meeting with Rostov, Viktor put on the raincoat and fedora Rostov was wearing and carried the Finnish guidebook with him as he boarded the train to Vyborg. In Vyborg, he left the clothing and the maps in the restroom thereby confusing the police about Rostov's whereabouts.

And Anon

A man in his sixties arrives in the Nizhny Novegorod Province with a simple travel bag after hiking for several days. He finds his way to an inn and asks for a room, but suggests he would like to eat first. Waiting in the little restaurant is the willowy actress at a table for two.

Analysis of Key Characters

in

A Gentleman in Moscow: A Novel

Count Alexander Ilyich Rostov

Count Rostov is set up to be the perfect hero. Despite being born and raised an aristocrat, he is likeable in the warm way he treats those outside his social class, and his lighthearted outlook on life despite the riches-to-rags predicament he finds himself in shows his strength of character. For many years, he has carried around the weight of his decisions and the resulting consequences (not being with his sister when she passed and his court ordered house arrest). It is not until he becomes accustomed to his life in the hotel that he humbly accepts his fate and recognizes his life's purpose. With his open-hearted and charismatic personality, it is easy to see why the other characters love and respect him. He is playful and youthful with young Nina and young Sofia; however, he is also a dignified gentleman who carries on intelligent conversations about literature and politics. He follows the rules of being a gentleman while also recognizing when and why it is necessary to play by his own rules at times. Ultimately, it is the relationships he forms and his loyalty to those around him that make him the hero of this novel.

Nina

Nina enters the story as a curious, intelligent young girl, but as the novel moves along, Nina grows more inwardly studious and serious. She quickly moves away from wanting to learn about princesses to developing hypotheses and testing them. When we encounter Nina as an adult, she is entirely focuses on the political movement and is too serious to stop and chat with her old friends from the hotel. Nina ultimately gives her time and energy to the cause, and eventually suffers because of it.

Sofia

Young Sofia is dropped off at the Metropol and placed in Rostov's care very unexpectedly. She is a quiet, inquisitive child, who adapts quickly to life in the hotel. While she is demure, she does enjoy her share of frivolity much to the delight of her father. Without her mother, her father plays the central role in her upbringing; however, the hotel staff and Anna play parts in bringing her into adulthood. With a gift for playing the piano, music and her father eventually open the doors of the hotel to the world.

Anna

An acclaimed actress who meets Rostov while her fame is on the rise. She is proud and bold and does not like to be told what to do. Unfortunately, Anna's fame fades overtime, and when Rostov meets her again, she is now much more humble and appreciative of kind gestures. As the novel progresses, their relationship does as well. She grows more loving, respectful, and motherly as time passes.

Major Symbols

in

A Gentleman in Moscow: A Novel

The desk of Grand Duke Demidov (his grandfather)

A symbol of status, wealth, and privilege, as well as family. Rostov chooses this desk to be moved to his small room because of what it symbolizes. He admires the craftmanship (which includes places to hide gold pieces) and the idea that countless hours of work by a gentleman took place here.

Essays of Michel de Montaigne

The book of Rostov's father that he aspires to read. At one point, the book is used to stabilize the desk; however, Rostov continues to return to the book in hopes of learning more about his father and how to be a parent himself. It is also this book that he destroys to hide secret information necessary for his escape.

Nina's passkey

Nina's passkey is a key to world of the hotel. Not only does the key literally open doors, it opens Rostov's eyes to all the intricacies and possibilities of life within the hotel.

Bread and salt

The Russian symbols for hospitality which are presented to Rostov's lifelong friend, Mishka, when he reappears after his stint with forced labor. Additionally, the title of Mishka's last project which is a compendium of the references to the word "Bread" in seminal texts. His breakdown and subsequent arrest is in response to his former editor wanting him to remove references to "bread" in Chekov's letters.

Bouillabaisse

This is the soup that the men are no are longer able to enjoy because the Russian government, famine and war have made it impossible to get all the required ingredients. For many years, the men dream of eating this soup again. When the day arrives that they have gathered all the ingredients, they celebrate by eating the soup. This triumvirate celebration solidifies their friendship and reminds them of life outside the Metropol with his flavors evocative of other countries.

Motifs

in

A Gentleman in Moscow: A Novel

Literature

Throughout the novel, Rostov, a well-read gentleman, alludes to several works of literature. He uses what he has learned from literary characters to help him understand his new life within the Metropol. His appreciation for reading is apparent in the way he uses literary characters as metaphors to describe various situations he finds himself in.

Music

One of Rostov's many loves is music. He has an ear for music. He can identify any note he recognizes in the hotel, like a chime or door closing. Beyond his knowledge and love of music, his daughter ends up with gift to play music by ear and is invited to join a traveling orchestra. Music, in the novel, always has a promising connotation.

Clocks/Time Passing/Chimes

In the novel, Rostov has a twice-chiming clock which he explains was his father's specifications to symbolize when one should be finished with his daily chores and when one should be in bed. One chime you should hear, and one you should not hear. In addition to Rostov's clock, readers will also notice several other references to clocks, time passing and chimes. For example, Rostov steals the Bishop's watch in his final escape plan and to aid the escape, all the hotel's phones ring (chime) at the same time.

The Fates

Rostov is a believer in the role of the Fates in his ordeals. The Fates are frequently references when serendipitous events occur. One key example is when it is noted that the Fates often send a guide to those who have lost their way just as Rostov has been sent Nina.

The Letter A

Each chapter of the novel begins with the letter A. Playful uses of alliteration and assonance occur with each title.

Themes

in

A Gentleman in Moscow: A Novel

Practicality and Spirit

The novel showcases the need to balance one's practical needs and the needs of one's spirit. Rostov knows to survive his life imprisonment in the hotel, he must be a master of practicalities and continue to nurture this spirit. His practical side is shown by mastering his schedule and continuing to keep up the most basic elements of life as a gentleman (a weekly trim, strict bedtimes, and exercise). However, it does not take Rostov long before he realizes that he will also need to nurture his spirit through literature, music, conversation, and fine cuisine. This theme is apparent through his practical bedroom assigned suite and his secret study designed for leisure.

Life's Purpose – Time and Place

Rostov adjusts to his new life in the Metropol, but he is still life considering his life's purpose. At one point, he feels he has become invisible; in another scene, he contemplates suicide. However, the entrance of three different women into the Metropol at three different times guide him to understanding his life's purpose. His young friend, Nina, becomes his guide to the hotel, and shows him how to view it as a country within itself. His lover, Anna, joins him in the Confederacy of the Humbled. Yet, it is his daughter, Sofia, who helps him identify his true purpose. He tells her that the only time in his life he knows he was in the right place at the right time for a distinct purpose is when her mother came to ask him to care for her. It is also Sofia who gives him the reason to escape.

Friendships with others outside his life's station

While Rostov forms quick relationships with those who grew up in privilege like him, his closest friendships are with those outside his life's station. His lover, Anna, grew up in poverty. He forms his strongest bonds in the hotel with Emile (a chef) and Andrey (the maître d). His relationship with the hotel handyman plays a pivotal role in his choices. Furthermore, his friendship with Osip begins because of their different life stations, and Osip comes to his aid more than once.

Discussion Questions

about

A Gentleman in Moscow: A Novel

Which character was your favorite? Why?

How does the influence of Russian literature resonate in Towles' work?

The popularity of novels, films, and television about the behind the scenes roles of people in lavish settings is on the rise. Why is it interesting to learn about the in's and outs of the Metropol? How does Towles create intrigue about the cuisine, seating charts, and place setting in the Boyarksy?

Upon learning Mishka wrote the poem from the beginning of the novel that sets everything into motion, how did this change your view of Mishka and Rostov?

How did you feel about the Bishop and his ever-changing positions in the hotel and his continued promotions? Why is he a perfect nemesis for Rostov?

What is the significance of the story of the peppered moths in relation to the novel?

Why does the author emphasize the scene with the glass in Casablanca?

Discuss the role of the women in the novel paying special attention to Rostov.

What are your feelings on the novel's ending?

Publication/Author Information

about

A Gentleman in Moscow: A Novel

A New York Times Bestseller and a Best Book of the Year by multiple publications, A Gentleman in Moscow was published in 2016 by Viking, An imprint of Penguin Random House. Amor Towles, the author, grew up in the Boston area. He earned an MA in English from Stanford University. Before becoming an author, he worked as an investment professional. His first novel, Rules of Civility, was also a bestseller and received high praise.

Other Books
by
Amor Towles

Rules of Civility, published in 2012, is Amor Towles' first novel about a woman who traverses the inner circles of New York high society in 1937. It delves into the intricacies of the city's upper echelon and takes the reader on a journey back to the old-world glitz and glamour of 1930s New York. Rules of Civility is a New York Times bestselling novel that has received praise from notable publications such as The Chicago Tribune, Wall Street Journal, and People magazine.

THANK YOU!

Brief Books pledges to always do our very best to produce high quality and entertaining material for you to enjoy. With that being said - the opinions, comments, criticisms, and compliments that we receive from fellow readers are always being taken to heart.

Take part to keep us going, add your review on Amazon and tell us and others what you think!

Sincerely,

Brief Books

71969127R00061

Made in the USA
San Bernardino, CA
20 March 2018